ADOLF HITLER

The Emergence of Nazism

Written by Xavier Leroy
In collaboration with Thomas Jacquemin
Translated by Rose Brichard

History 50MINUTES.com

ADOLF HITLER   1

BIOGRAPHY   3

Paternal influences

Hitler, the failed artist

Four years at war

Infiltrating the German Workers' Party

Rise to power

The first signs of war

Total war

Defeat and death

CONTEXT   21

From one war to the next: the humiliating Treaty of Versailles

Growing power

HIGHLIGHTS   25

Fascism: Nazism's elder brother

The advent of the Third Reich

German territorial expansion

The age of conquest

The destruction of an entire population

In the heat of battle

Impact

Summary

FIND OUT MORE   47

ADOLF HITLER

- **Born:** 20 April 1889 in Braunau am Inn, Austria
- **Died:** 30 April 1945 in Berlin
- **Key information:**
  - He organised the National Socialist German Workers' Party (NSDAP)
  - He installed a totalitarian political regime in Germany
  - He is responsible for starting WWII
  - He is responsible for the 20th century's biggest genocide

Hitler is the 20th century's most controversial figure. His name alone conjures images of the greatest horrors of our time. Yet there was nothing to suggest that this Austrian man was fated to such a shocking and historic destiny. He was passionate about art and hoped to make a career out of it, but was rejected from his attempts to pursue this field of study several times. This gave way to a dark period of his life, spent reading works which would radicalise his thinking and change the course of his life forever. A few years later, he left Austria and headed to Germany, a country whose power he admired. In 1914, he fought in WWI and showed great zeal in battle, but was injured in combat. He learned of Germany's defeat on his sickbed. He was certain that this outcome was due to enemies working within the German nation itself: Jews and communists. On Hitler's return to health, he was greeted by a country which had been plunged into chaos by the humiliating Treaty of Versailles. It was then that he joined the National Socialist German Workers'

Party and quickly rose through its ranks, reorganising its structures and becoming its leader. His ambitions went far beyond this; he planned to captain a whole new civilisation and protect Aryan purity; he would stop at nothing to achieve this goal. Despite his failed coup against the state in 1923, he was determined to rise to the top and lead the country, and Germany's disastrous political condition at the time helped him do so. He appointed himself as Head of State and, led by his ideological convictions, used this as a platform for organising the most shocking crimes against humanity of modern history. In his wake, he would leave only ashes and blood.

BIOGRAPHY

Portrait of Adolf Hitler, dated 1933

PATERNAL INFLUENCES

Hitler came into the world on 20 April 1889 in Braunau am Inn, a small town in present-day Austria not far from the German border. His father Alois Hitler (1837-1902) worked as part of the border control, and had two children other than from a previous marriage. In 1885 Alois married his third wife, his younger cousin Klara Pöllz (1860-1907). From this marriage, their son Adolf was born, as well as two other children: Edmond in 1895 and Paula in 1896.

HITLER'S COMPLEX FAMILY LINEAGE

Adolf Hitler may well have been called by a different name. For much of his life, his father Alois went by his mother's surname (Maria Schicklgruber, 1795-1847) since his own father's identity was unknown. Five years after Alois' birth, his mother married a blue-collar worker named Georg Hiedler (1792-1857). When Alois was just ten years old, his mother died and he was taken into the care of Johann Hiedler (1808-1888), Georg's brother. In 1876, Johann made Alois his heir by claiming that he was in fact Georg's son. It was for this reason that Alois adopted the surname Hiedler, which became Hitler over time and through mistaken transcription. Historians are still unsure whether this name-change reflects a genuine paternal link or was merely aimed at ensuring someone could carry on the family name. In any case, it has been noted that it was probably a great help to Hitler's career - can you imagine crowds of people rallying to the cry "Heil Schicklgruber!"?

Hitler's childhood was spent moving between different locations due to his father's work. His father was very proud of his career and the elevated social status which came with it, harbouring great hopes that his son would follow in his footsteps. However, the young Adolf had other ideas. At school, he was thought to be an intelligent but lazy pupil, who only worked hard in the subjects he was interested in. One of these was art and design, and he seriously considered pursuing an artistic career. This dream was met with hostility from his father and their relationship quickly descended into frequent and violent arguments. This rift was never healed and Alois died on 3 January 1903.

WAS HITLER OF JEWISH DESCENT?

While Georg Hiedler is Hitler's legal grandfather, nothing regarding his lineage is certain. Many rumours about the true identity of Maria Schricklgruber's lover have circulated; among these is a theory which suggests Hitler's grandfather was in fact Jewish. When Maria fell pregnant she was working as a housekeeper in Graz for a Jewish family, the Frankenbergers. Rumour has it that she had an affair with the family's oldest son, however no trace of a family with this name in Graz has been found. Other theories suggest that Maria worked for the Rothschilds in Vienna.

Hitler himself organised several secret investigations into this sensitive question, but no concrete answers could be found. Fearing for the integrity of his anti-Semitic convictions, Hitler got rid of all trace of his father's identity so that no-one could discover the truth, whatever it may have been.

HITLER, THE FAILED ARTIST

Hitler continued his schooling in Linz without any great conviction, but here in Linz the teenage Hitler began taking great interest in novels, history books and opera. Before graduating in 1907, he convinced his mother to let him pursue a more artistic field of study in Vienna. He rented a student room and enrolled in the Academy of Fine Art, but was rejected in the entry examinations. He then discovered that architecture was his real passion but was unable to enrol in this degree discipline since he did not have the correct qualifications.

Towards the end of 1907, Hitler's mother Klara was diagnosed with breast cancer. Despite medical intervention, she died on 23 December. At the beginning of the following year, Hitler returned to Vienna with his friend August who was a student at the conservatoire. In September, Hitler tried once again to win a place at the Academy of Fine Arts, and was once again rejected. Unable to admit his failure, he broke off all contact with his friends and found himself forced to live in homeless shelters, anonymous and desperate. This was a very difficult period of his life. He did his best to survive on Vienna's streets on his orphan's benefits and casual work, with help from charities. During 1910 his situation improved as he began painting post-cards and selling them in the street.

Despite his somewhat desperate situation, Hitler did everything to keep up appearances and present the world with the image of a misunderstood rather than failed artist. He was still passionate about opera, and happy to go hungry in order to save enough money to see a performance. It was around this time that he took up reading again with a renewed interest in geopolitics and European history. He greatly admired Germany and its power, feeling only contempt toward the carefree Austrian attitude. Embittered by his own failure, Hitler began prescribing to an increasingly radical political ideology and became overtly anti-Semitic. In his eyes, Jewish people were responsible for all of Europe's problems, including his own.

WHY DID HITLER BECOME ANTI-SEMITIC?

Some of the trickiest questions to approach about this controversial figure are those concerning the roots of his anti-Semitism. According to many historians, a hatred strong enough to inspire genocide could only have been developed through a particularly unfortunate episode of his life involving one or more Jews. Though many theories on the topic have been proposed, none of them have been proven. While it is generally agreed that Hitler's radical political thought has its roots in Vienna, there is no consensus on whether or not it is linked to a specific event. In fact, the research shows quite the opposite of what may be expected; it seems that Hitler maintained favourable relations with the Jewish people he mixed with.

Nowadays, several historians believe that Hitler's anti-Semitism instead stems from political opportunism after the war, when he saw the Jewish population as a politically valuable scapegoat to aid his rise to power; if he framed them as the enemy he could show himself to be the saviour of the German nation. This theory stems from the fact that most of what is known about Hitler's life in Vienna comes from his own writings, which he could very well have distorted to present himself in a certain light. It should be noted that at this time many works which posited the supremacy of certain races over others were indeed in circulation. Furthermore, in Germany's case, anti-Semitism was fuelled by the use of Jews as a scapegoat for the collapse of the German and Austro-Hungarian Empires.

In May 1913, Hitler left Vienna and went to live in Munich. This decision was based not only on admiration for Germany but on a desire to escape his Austrian military service responsibilities. That notwithstanding, the Austrian authorities managed to locate him the following year and force him to return to Linz. He then underwent medical testing to have himself declared unfit for duty, therefore finding himself free to return to Munich where he was to learn news which would change the course of his life forever: WWI had begun.

FOUR YEARS AT WAR

While Europe had been largely peaceful for several decades, the continent had harboured growing political tensions since the beginning of the 20th century. Several hegemonic powers formed alliances such as the Triple Alliance between Germany, Austria-Hungary, and Italy and the Triple Entente between Great Britain, France and Russia. The purpose of these coalitions was to ensure collective defence, whereby a country's allies would declare war on the opponent in solidarity if it were to be attacked.

On 28 June 1914, the heir to the Austro-Hungarian throne Franz Ferdinand (1863-1914) and his wife were assassinated by a Yugoslav nationalist during their visit to Sarajevo. Considering Serbia equally guilty of this crime, Austria sent the Serbian king an ultimatum which he refused. Therefore, Austria declared war on 28 July. France and Russia supported Serbia and Germany came to Austria's aid. When Germany invaded Belgium, Britain intervened in light of Belgium's declared neutrality. Italy chose to remain neutral while the Ottoman Empire joined forces with Germany in the following months.

Fervently pro-German, Hitler gained permission to enlist in the Bavarian Army and served on the French front in October 1914. While he received limited military training before entering into combat, he showed himself to be a brave and zealous soldier. He was quick to help injured comrades and maintained a high morale throughout. This was to earn him the prestigious Iron Cross as well as a promotion to the rank of corporal. In October 1918, his unit was attacked with mustard gas and though he was not killed, he was temporarily blinded which put him out of action for the rest of the war. It was during his recovery in hospital that he learned of Germany's defeat. He was shocked and troubled by the news.

Photo of Hitler with other German soldiers during WWI

The final peace treaty was signed at Versailles, and Germany was humiliated. The country was forced to accept the terms of a treaty which identified it as the only nation at fault regarding the start of the war. The terms of the treaty saw Germany committed to paying huge war reparations, giving up all its colonies, ceding parts of its territory to the victors and strictly limiting the size of its army.

INFILTRATING THE GERMAN WORKERS' PARTY

On his return to Germany, Hitler found the country in a state of total chaos. The empire had become a republic which lacked legitimacy. German communists capitalised on this situation and tried to take power by force, calling upon the *Freikorps* - units of former soldiers - for help. After several months of civil war, the country became stable once again. These events fuelled Hitler's suspicions that Germany's defeat was the result of enemies hidden within - communists and Jewish people.

Hitler was still a member of the army and was renowned for his political knowledge. For these reasons, he was recruited to work as an intelligence agent. His duties were to monitor small extremist groups, and it was in this vein that Hitler was sent to infiltrate the German Workers' Party, a small nationalist party. At the beginning, he played the role of spectator but quickly stood out in party meetings to the extent that the party's leader Anton Drexler (1884-1942) asked him to join their ranks. Hitler accepted the offer with his superiors' permission.

As a member, Hitler drastically changed the small party's organisational structures, and soon became one of the party's directors before being appointed as its leader in July 1921. He boosted the party's communications, buying a newspaper and renaming his party as the National Socialist German Workers' Party (NSDAP), also to be known as the Nazi Party as an abbreviation of the German *nationalso-*

zialistisch. Under Hitler's leadership, party membership numbers grew significantly as did the movement's overall credibility. His plan for the party was simple: take power using force if necessary, officially denounce the Treaty of Versailles, get rid of Jews and communists and restore Germany to its former glory.

In January 1923, due to crippling debt, Germany decided to stop paying its war reparations. France and Belgium sent troops to occupy the industrial Rhineland region which plunged the country into the depths of a true crisis. The situation became steadily worse, and Hitler thought the time was right to launch a *coup d'état* in Munich. However, he had been counting on the army's support to achieve this; the opposite outcome prevailed and the Nazi leaders were arrested. In March 1924 Hitler and his comrades were charged with treason, but received only short jail sentences in Landsberg prison. From his jail cell, Hitler reflected on his political future and came to the realisation that he would have to use the law to his advantage to reach his goals. He also dictated what would become his autobiography *Mein Kampf* to Rudolf Hess (1894-1987), his deputy. He was re-leased on parole in December 1925 though was banned from public-speaking. The ban was lifted in March 1927 and in February 1926, and the Nazi Party's reformation and return to action was authorised.

RISE TO POWER

Hitler was aware that in order to succeed he had to rally support from not only the lowest and most disadvantaged strata of society, but the middle classes and several leading figures of industry and finance. As such, he decided to present a less violent image and tone down his political discourse. While the Nazi party saw its membership increase, they were unsuccessful in the 1928 elections, and for good reason; the situation in Germany had improved and the people were therefore less inclined to get behind Hitler's policies. Everything changed in 1929 when the stock market crash ripped through Germany and left the country with a collapsed economy and skyrocketing levels of unemployment. With the traditional political parties unable to adequately address the crisis, the electorate turned towards other parties who proposed more radical solutions. It was under these circumstances that the Nazis received 18% of the vote in the September 1930 federal election.

NSDAP meeting in 1930, attended by Hitler

Two years later, Hitler announced his presidential candidacy for the election which was eventually won by Paul von Hindenburg (1847-1934). Hitler's party became the most popular in the country with 37% of the vote in July, before dropping again later in the year. Franz von Papen (1879-1969), a member of the Catholic Party, proposed a coalition government between the two parties. Hitler accepted on the condition that he be appointed Chancellor; von Papen agreed.

In the wake of the *Reichstag* (German parliament) fire, Hitler took the opportunity to denounce the dangers of Communism, claiming that the fire had in fact been an attempted Communist coup. He was therefore granted the power to rule by decree. From there, he introduced a series of laws to help facilitate his grand project. On 23 March, he rose to a level of absolute power before declaring that the NSDAP was the only legal party in July. On 2 August, after President Hindenburg's death, Hitler established the Third Reich. To guard against any dissent, he put extreme forces of repression in place and equipped the state with an ideological indoctrination system. All Germans had to submit to this indoctrination system to show their loyalty to and acceptance of Nazi ideology, whereas the repressive forces were targeted at potential dissidents and those he saw as obstacles to his programme of Aryan purification. This programme of repression saw the first concentration camps established.

THE FIRST SIGNS OF WAR

Hitler's next goal was territorial expansion, and he implemented policies which would help him secure the space needed for Germany's development. In this area too he went from strength to strength, managing to reabsorb Saarland into German borders and annex Sudetenland by occupying Rhineland. With no reaction from the Allied powers, Hitler was ready to take on Poland. Determined to reach Eastern Prussia, Germany asked for Poland's permission to pass through its territory; this request was refused. Hitler therefore ordered troops to invade and occupy Poland on 1 September 1939. Unable to accept such an affront, the Allies demanded that Hitler recall his troops. He refused and the invasion continued. On 3 September, France and Britain declared war.

Fighting began in Norway and Denmark from April 1940, with both countries soon falling to the Nazis. The following month, Hitler's next target was France which was to be reached through Belgium. Belgium was quickly defeated, along with the Netherlands and Luxemburg. In only a few days, the *Werhmacht* (the Third Reich's army) crushed Allied forces; France was the last man standing. In order to avoid all-out invasion, the French Head of State Marshal Pétain (1856-1951) asked for an armistice, which was signed on 20 May.

<u>**HITLER: A TRUE STRATEGIST OR JUST AN AMATEUR?**</u>

In defeating France, Hitler erased all trace of Germany's humiliation in the Treaty of Versailles and showed himself to be a true warlord. However, to what extent was he responsible for this success? Was he truly skilled as a military strategist? While he had significant experience of combat, he was certainly not a professional strategist. He never held a strategic position in the army, nor did he receive any formal military training in the area. Any knowledge he possessed was self-taught. Despite these factors, he did not hesitate in declaring himself as head of all armed forces and demanding that he should be consulted on all strategy decisions. Though he was an amateur, he was more than an incompetent lunatic - as he was described in several post-war testimonies. He was intelligent, had a good memory and good technical knowledge. All of this helped him to correctly grasp the situation at hand. While he is not entirely responsible for the plans which secured Nazi victories during the first years of conflict, he nevertheless had the intuition to listen to the advice from his best generals, despite many sceptics' fears that he would do the opposite.

In any case, his good judgement was not to last. Nazi failure in the Battle of Moscow in December 1941 damaged his relations with his generals. Hitler became increasingly uncompromising, scornful and incredulous, unable to tolerate any opinions which went against his own. He started making decisions without consulting his officers and anyone who tried to reason with him was met with his terrible fits of rage and put their job on the line in doing so. At the end of the war, there was a complete schism between a delusional Hitler and his level-headed officers, who knew all too well that the war was a lost cause.

TOTAL WAR

With France defeated, Hitler marked out Soviet Russia, which he considered as Germany's natural enemy, as his next target. His offensive against the USSR began on 22 June 1941, and had initial success. However, it lasted for longer than expected and since Hitler had refused to give his troops warm winter clothes, the freezing cold quickly brought them to a stand-still.

Meanwhile, Japan decided to capitalise on Europe's explosive events and attack the American naval base at Pearl Harbour on 7 December 1941. This led to America entering into war, and Hitler in turn declared war on the USA just a few days later.

Hitler was aware that the clock was ticking; it was essential to defeat the USSR before America became truly involved. Hitler launched a major offensive in the Caucasus and Stalingrad in order to seize Soviet oil fields and destroy Stalin's (1878-1953) flagship industry which also bore his name. While everything appeared to go exactly to plan in Hitler's eyes, the situation eventually declined when Soviet troops led a counter-attack and annihilated the German troops in Stalingrad. The situation in Africa was no less catastrophic; British troops had come to block the German attempt to seize territories and the German soldiers were forced to abandon their efforts.

DEFEAT AND DEATH

In early 1944, the German military found itself in a truly critical situation. The Wehrmacht was in steep decline and the Allies were instigating a series of missions to reclaim lost territories. Europe was being gradually liberated and by the end of the year, the Allies were knocking at the door of the Third Reich. With Hitler undeterred and determined to continue fighting until the bitter end, some of his officers tried in vain to assassinate him, knowing that his plans would lead to a total defeat and wanting to negotiate with the Allies.

A SERIES OF ATTEMPTS ON HITLER'S LIFE

Hitler made many enemies throughout his political career, however there were relatively few attempts to assassinate him. The first attempt took place on 8 November 1939. According to yearly tradition, Hitler celebrated the Beer Hall Putsch of 1923 in a restaurant in Munich. However, he left earlier than usual. Not long after his departure a bomb exploded and destroyed half of the restaurant. The police soon found the culprit: a workman named Georg Esler who claimed to have acted alone.

Other attempts on his life were made by members of the military. Some army officers were quick to recognise the threat Hitler represented, but the victories achieved under his rule until 1941 discouraged them from taking action. However, things began to change in 1942; a German victory seemed increasingly unlikely and the regime's crimes came to light. It was not until March 1943 that their assassination plans finally materialised. On 13 March, Hitler took a flight to the Russian front. Before his departure, an officer planted a bomb on board, but it never exploded. Another officer plotted a suicide attack for the 20th when Hitler was visiting Berlin. However, it was doomed to failure since Hitler cut short his visit. The last assassination attempt took place on 20 July 1944, when Colonel von Stauffenberg planted a briefcase with a bomb in it in the briefing room of Hitler's East Prussian headquarters. Though the bomb did indeed explode, Hitler survived the attack and everyone involved was arrested and executed.

In December 1944, Hitler risked everything and launched a new offensive in the Ardennes which failed. His empire was on the brink of collapse. He took his anger out on his generals and ordered that German resistance continue, but nothing could stop the Allies invading his country. In April 1945, the war was close to its end. Hitler locked himself in his Berlin bunker where he hoped to stay until the very end. The Soviets surrounded the town and gradually invaded. He refused to be captured alive, and shot himself on 30 April 1945. His successor Karl Dönitz (1891-1980) took on the responsibility of officially surrendering on 8 May.

<u>What happened to Hitler's body?</u>

Hitler had expressed the wish that his body did not fall into enemy hands. Therefore, German soldiers took his corpse out of the bunker, burned it and buried his remains in a bomb crater. The Soviets nonetheless managed to locate them, and had them secretly transported to the USSR to be identified. It was only after Stalin's death and the release of the last German prisoners of war that the exact circumstances of Hitler's death were made public. Rumour has it that his skull is kept in the Kremlin's archives.

CONTEXT

FROM ONE WAR TO THE NEXT: THE HUMILIA-TING TREATY OF VERSAILLES

Conditions in Germany became unbearable from 1918 onwards. Soldiers and civilians alike were completely demoralised and the country was plagued by famine and strikes. In early autumn, the Allied armies launched a general offensive which crushed the German army. Certain that they would not be able to recover, German generals convinced Emperor William II (1859-1941) to reach a peace agreement with the Allies before they penetrated the German borders. Having been granted imperial permission, German officers were sent to negotiate with the Triple Entente's representatives who agreed to a temporary ceasefire. This was followed by discussions of a peace treaty; the Allies made it clear that the restrictions imposed upon Germany would be significant.

Meanwhile in Berlin, the Kaiser abdicated and the empire became a socialist-dominated republic. When the military learned of the Versailles Treaty's terms, it refused to accept responsibility for the peace negotiations, forcing politicians to step up and take the blame. The army even marched in the streets of Berlin in to show that it was still fit for battle and that this humiliating surrender was effected without its consent through the betrayal of hidden enemies within its ranks. Many Germans put their faith in this account of the tale, and Hitler would use this myth as the ideational foundation for his political movement.

German troops return to Berlin

GROWING POWER

After the Treaty of Versailles was signed on 28 June 1919, the situation in Germany went from bad to worse. Due to France and Belgium's occupation of the Rhineland, an industrial region of Germany, inflation in the German economy spiralled out of control. Hitler saw this as an opportunity to launch a coup known as the Beer Hall Putsch which ended in in failure. He developed his new strategy during several months spent in jail as a result.

When he was freed in 1925, he began putting his plans into action, playing down the most extreme elements of his ideology in order to establish himself as a respectable leader and gain national success for the Nazi Party. At first, these efforts only wielded minor results; the Nazi Party continued to grow but this growth was not translated to electoral success. Their ascent to power was somewhat blocked by the German economic recovery, which was largely facilitated by American investment.

During this period, two of the most important Nazi organisations first appeared:

- The *Schutzstaffel* (Protection Squadron), more commonly known as the SS, was created in April 1925 with Heinrich Himmler (1900-1945) at the helm. It was a unit of elites whose members had to meet strict racial and ideological requirements. The organisation's initial purpose was to ensure Hitler's personal protection. After the Nazis came to power in 1933, the power and influence of the SS grew exponentially. It was responsible for creating concentration camps as centres of deportation for all enemies of the new regime. During WWII, the SS developed an armed wing called the *Waffen-SS* which exerted control over forced labourers from occupied countries. By the end of the conflict, the SS had become a political and military power in its own right.
- The *Sicherheitsdienst* (Security Service), more commonly known as the SD. In May 1931, Himmler met a young man newly recruited to the Nazi Party named Reinhard Heydrich (1904-1942). He was a former member of the navy who had been dismissed for bad behaviour, and Himmler gave him the duty of creating a Nazi intelligence agency. He got to work quickly and in July 1932 the SD was created. Its mission was to expose any spies within the

ranks of the party and to gather intelligence on political enemies.

Germany's economic situation returned to chaos in 1929 in the wake of the Wall Street crash. From early 1930, bankruptcies became commonplace and unemployment reached record heights. Hitler became popular among the electorate in these turbulent times and his party became the biggest in the country, earning 37% of the votes in July 1932. Despite this, his path to power remained firmly blocked. Furthermore, in the November elections the party suffered losses and some of its financial backers defected to other parties. Things improved for Hitler when Franz von Papen, a member of the Catholic Party, opened negotiations with the Nazi Party and other small nationalist groups in the hope of establishing a coalition government. Hitler agreed to the proposition on the condition that he would be appointed chancellor. President Hindenburg agreed to this, and Hitler formed his new government.

HIGHLIGHTS

FASCISM: NAZISM'S ELDER BROTHER

When Hitler was restructuring the German Workers' Party, he was largely inspired by a major political figure of the time - Benito Mussolini (1833-1945). A former socialist journalist, Mussolini had formed his own extremist party - Italian Fascist Party - in 1919. Hitler used this as a model for his NSDAP. He chose the Swastika as the symbol of Nazism, an emblem that had been used by Germanic tribes for thousands of years, and introduced the Nazi salute which was inspired by the Roman salute.

SA troops saluting Hitler in 1932

Just as the Italian Fascist Party had its Blackshirts, Hitler formed a political militia known as the SA (*Sturmabteilug* - Storm Battalion) which were nicknamed the Brownshirts due to the colour of their uniforms. Their goal was to protect Nazi Party meetings and disrupt those of political enemies. Following Mussolini's example, Hitler was happy to resort to violence especially with regards to communists, often leading to violence on the streets.

Those who would become the most prominent figures of Nazism joined the movement when the NSDAP was formed. Among them were Ernst Röhm (1887-1934), German army captain and a senior Freikorps member, Hermann Goering (1893-1946) former member of the German air force, journalist Josef Goebbels (1897-1945), and agronomist Heinrich Himmler.

After his failed coup, the imprisoned Hitler devoted himself to developing his political programme as outlined in his book *Mein Kampf*. This work is both an autobiography and a detailed explanation of his objectives, tackling the major elements of Hitler's political philosophy. These are:

- Pan-Germanism: the idea of unifying all peoples from Germanic cultures under one central authority.
- *Lebensraum*: living space for the German race. Germany had no room to expand, as such it must colonise Eastern Europe.
- Racial supremacy: Germans are the descendants of Aryans, a mythical race who lived in Europe several millennia ago, said to have founded the most advanced civilization of their time. Due to this lineage, the Nazis considered Germans as a distinct race - genetically supe-

rior and destined to rule over other cultures, particularly those to the East.

- Racial purity: to ensure the survival of the Aryan race and preserve its genetic heritage, the German race must get rid of all parasitic elements through strict segregation. Hitler considered Jewish people, Communists, the Tzigane people, homosexuals, Jehovah's Witnesses, nd the disabled as "parasites". If segregation was insufficient, they should be eliminated.
- *Führerprinzip* (leader principle): to successfully implement these measures, Germany must be governed by one man only, possessed of absolute political power and authority. Any disobedience to the Fuhrer's orders would be considered treason.

THE ADVENT OF THE THIRD REICH

Though Hitler became German chancellor on 30 January 1933, this was not the most secure position. His coalition government only featured two Nazis in addition to himself, and his quick downfall seemed likely. In an almost theatrical twist, the Reichstag burned down on 27 February. Framing this as a communist coup d'état, Hitler obtained Hindenburg's permission to rule by decree - unchecked by parliament - and suspend individual freedoms. He used this power to make the Communist party illegal and intimidate the parties which were hostile towards him and his policies. On the 23rd of March parliament awarded him absolute power and several days later, Hitler made trade unions illegal and created a political police force called the Gestapo (abbreviation of *Geheime Staatspolizei* - Secret

State Police). In July, the NSDAP became the only legal party. In September, the media and cultural institutions came into the firing line.

WHO SET FIRE TO THE REICHSTAG?

This question is still subject to debate. At the time, the Nazis accused the Communists of setting fire to the Reichstag after one of their members, Marinus van der Lubbe (1909-1934) was found at the scene of the crime. Immediately, the Hungarian communist leaders who were present in the country at the time were also implicated and put on trial as co-defendants alongside Van der Lubbe. However, the evidence was insufficient and only Van der Lubbe was convicted and sentenced to death. Given that the Reichstag was too large for one man acting alone to undertake such an operation, another theory which links the fire to the Nazi party has been proposed. Many have speculated that members of the party were involved in the crime or even that a secret tunnel linking the Reichstag and the Prussian ministerial palace existed; at the time of the incident, Hermann Goering was at the palace. Unfortunately, most witness accounts disappeared during the war, which means the case is still unsolved and remains a mystery.

Hitler was finally in a position of absolute power, but the road to his grand project was still littered with minor obstacles. The first of these was none other than President Hindenburg who was himself a threat since he had the legal capacity to mobilise the army against the government. However, he was very unwell and his days were numbered. The other obstacle was an organisation which Hitler himself had established - the SA. SA members showed signs of extreme discontent with the situation, demanding a true revolution and making Hitler fear the worst. Hitler was aware of the key position the army held on the political scene, and therefore negotiated with one of the German army's leaders. He promised to get rid of the Nazis who refused to toe the line if the army allowed Hitler to assume Hindenburg's position in addition to his own without conducting elections. Therefore, as promised, Hitler began a purge on his own party on 30 June 1934 in what is known as the night of the long knives. Röhm and his adherents, as well as the Nazis' most dangerous political opponents, were all killed. On 2 August, Hindenburg died and Hitler became both President and Commander in Chief of the armed forces; the German republic was from that moment succeeded by the Third Reich.

SA troops parade in front of Hitler, 1935.

Under the new Third Reich regime, Hitler had to carefully guard against any potential uprising and used oppression and indoctrination to do so. In this vein, all of the country's security services were brought together under one umbrella organisation: the *Reichssicherheitshauptamt* (Reich Main Security Office), more commonly known as the RSHA, which was directed by Heydrich under Himmler. This organisation's purpose was to keep track of anyone and everyone who was likely to challenge the new regime. To eliminate any potential threats, the Nazis built prison camps, more commonly known as concentration camps, where enemies of the regime were detained without trial. The first camp opened in Dachau as soon as Hitler came to power, and many others were to follow in the months after. Concentration camps were Himmler's responsibility, and he made sure that every camp was guarded by the SS. Living conditions in the camps were atrocious; prisoners lived in wooden huts, received minimal amounts of food and had no hygiene facilities. In addition to this, they were constantly subjected to violence from the camp guards.

All Germans were indoctrinated into Nazism from a very young age. Hitler banned all youth organisations except one: the Hitler Youth. All children were forced to adhere to the organisation, in the hope that they would be moulded into perfect citizen-soldiers through their education on Nazi ideology and physical exercise. They were also instilled with a sense of loyalty to the Fuhrer, the supremacy of the German race and hatred towards all its supposed enemies.

Hitler posing with three children

GERMAN TERRITORIAL EXPANSION

Having firmly established his position at the national level, Hitler turned towards foreign policy in order to eradicate the

Treaty of Versailles and its consequences. He began this with a public announcement of rearmament, something which completely violated the terms of the treaty. In January 1935, he re-annexed Saarland, a region which Germany had been forced to cede under the terms of the Treaty of Versailles. He then sent troops to occupy the Rhineland region, another territorial region which was forcibly demilitarised under the treaty in March 1936. Two years later, Germany annexed Austria and in November of the same year, Hitler negotiated with France and Britain to annex Sudetenland, a German-speaking region of Czechoslovakia. In March 1939, he set about dismantling what remained of Czechoslovakia, annexing the Czech region to Germany and establishing the Slovak region as a German satellite country. Germany also claimed the Memel Territory in Lithuania.

AUSTRIA AND THE CONCILIATION ATTEMPTS

In both France and Britain, governments sought to avoid starting a war with Germany at all costs, which explains their initial lack of military response to Hitler's actions. Instead they protested verbally.

In 1937, Neville Chamberlain (1869-1940) was elected as British Prime Minister and promoted a peaceful approach to foreign policy, particularly with regards to the Third Reich. It was during Chamberlain's time that Hitler annexed Sudetenland, a German-speaking region of Czechoslovakia. This was in spite of the Czechoslovak government - allied with France and Britain - categorically refusing to cede this territory.

The political tensions mounted and war seemed likely. In the knowledge that their armies were not ready for war, Chamberlain and his French counterpart Édouard Daladier (1884-1970) decided to negotiate the annexation of Sudetenland with Hitler. The territory was awarded to Germany on the condition that German territorial expansion would end there. Hitler accepted this compromise, and signed the Munich Agreement on 29 and 30 September 1939; the Czechoslovak government did not take part. Chamberlain and Daladier were sure that they had secured lasting peace. In fact, this peace was only fleeting and Hitler continued to annex neighbouring territories through brutal intimidation. In both London and Paris, it became clear that force would have to be used to stop Hitler in his tracks.

THE AGE OF CONQUEST

The Allied powers' lack of response left Hitler confident that attacking Poland carried little risk. As such, in the summer of 1939, he exerted pressure on Poland to allow Germany to use its territory as a passage to East Prussia. Poland, having recently established a link with Great Britain and France, firmly refused Germany's proposal. Meanwhile, the Western powers opened discussions with the USSR to negotiate military support in the case of war. However, both Poland and the UK had little faith in Russia, and the discussions soon ended. As such, Stalin engaged in secret negotiations with Germany and found common ground around Poland, a country which both states sought to claim. Neither Poland

nor Germany was ready to engage in battle with one another and therefore a secret non-aggression pact was signed
which would last for five years. It established Soviet and
German spheres of influence in Eastern Europe and divided
Poland between the two states.

Strengthened by this pact with the USSR and convinced
that the Allies would yet again fail to intervene, Germany
invaded Poland on 1 September 1939. This time however,
the Allies reacted, sending an ultimatum to Berlin which
stipulated that if Hitler did not withdraw his troops from
Poland, France and Britain would declare war. Hitler was
convinced that the Allies were bluffing and continued the
offensive. Therefore, on 3 September both the British and
French governments declared war on Germany, heralding
the dawn of WWII.

The invasion of Poland, September 1939

The Allies' armies were not ready for combat, meaning

Hitler had all the time in the world to finish what he had started in Poland. Poland fell to the Nazis within a few weeks. This began a period known as the Phoney War during which troops were deployed from both sides of the Franco-German border, but no true offensive was ever launched. During the Phoney War, Hitler tried to negotiate with the Allies to no avail; he would have to obtain peace through military action.

THE BERLIN-ROME-TOKYO AXIS

Hitler knew that in order to emerge victorious from conflict against the countries which won the last war he would need allies. Ideologically, Germany's closest ally was fascist Italy. Already in 1934 Hitler tried to establish ties with Italy, but Mussolini was not his biggest fan. He thought of Hitler as an extremist version of himself and did not agree with the notions of racial supremacy and anti-Semitism which were so key to Hitler's philosophy. Mussolini initially thought it preferable to establish favourable relations with France and Britain and combat German expansion. However, in 1936 when Italy began its conquest of Ethiopia, Italy received neither France nor Britain's support and was subject to economic sanctions imposed by the League of Nations. Italy had only one way to turn: towards Nazi Germany. On 1 November 1936, the two dictators established the Rome-Berlin Axis which formalised cooperation between the two countries, strengthened further by the 1939 Pact of Steel which established a military alliance, signed on 22 May. Japan entered into the axis on 27 September 1940, making it a tripartite pact.

In April 1940, the Allies readied themselves for military intervention in Norway in order to cut off Germany's supply of Swedish iron, a material vital to the Nazi war effort. Hitler pre-empted the Allies' intervention by invading Norway and Germany and a bloody battle between the Nazis and the Allies ensued. Both sides suffered considerable losses but eventually the Allies were forced to retreat. In May, Hitler set his sights on France and decided to attack. Just as in 1914, the German army marched through Belgium and invaded the Netherlands and Luxemburg in one fell swoop. Hoping to use the element of surprise, Hitler sent armoured divisions to struggle through rough terrain of the Ardennes region, considered an impossible feat for this type of military unit. The manoeuvre was a complete success - in the space of a few days, the Allied armies were caught in a trap. To avoid an outright invasion, the French government led by Philippe Pétain proposed an armistice which was signed on 20 May. Hitler was jubilant - in only a few months his troops had conquered five countries including a global power.

Furthermore, Hitler was sure that Britain was soon likely to negotiate a peace deal, finding itself alone in the face of Nazism. However, in May the British government was taken over by Winston Churchill (1874-1965) who was resolutely anti-Nazi in his convictions. Churchill did not respond to Hitler's attempts to broker peace with the UK, leading to a huge Nazi air offensive against known as the Battle of Britain

(August-September 1940). Despite its inferior equipment and technology, Britain emerged victorious.

Having defeated France, Hitler turned his attention towards a country which he considered to be Germany's natural enemy - Soviet Russia. He targeted the USSR partly due to his lack of confidence in the non-aggression pact signed between the two states and partly due to the vast reserves of raw materials it possessed. However, before Nazi Germany could devote itself to the fight against Communism, it was forced to come to the aid of Italy as it struggled to establish a presence in Greece and Egypt. In March 1941, Germany sent troops to support the Italian forces in Libya and conquer Greece and Yugoslavia, the latter being allied with Britain. With the southern flank secured, Hitler was ready to instigate his invasion of the USSR. The offensive was launched on 22 June 1941 and was met with unexpected results. Over the course of the following months, thousands of the Wehrmacht were taken prisoner but they eventually made it to the edge of Moscow. However, winter arrived and caused irreparable damage. Hitler had assumed that the USSR would not hold out past autumn, so the troops had made no provisions for a Russian winter. As such, the German troops struggled to fight against Soviet attacks, unable to bear the cold and sustaining significant losses. Nevertheless, they stood their ground.

THE DESTRUCTION OF AN ENTIRE POPULATION

In parallel to these military offensives, Hitler was fighting another battle. He had long harboured a vision of eliminating Europe's Jewish population; the first step in his plan was a legal segregation of Jews from all other peoples. From April 1933 onwards, Jews were no longer allowed to hold public office, and two years later the Nuremberg laws came into force. These stripped Jews of citizenship, banned them from mixing with Germans and forced them to wear a distinctive emblem - the Star of David. Following on from this, the Nazi government tried to force the Jewish population to flee the country by deporting many to concentration camps, confiscating their property and inflicting violence with increasing frequency. Despite all of this, many Jews remained in Germany.

When Hitler ordered the invasion of the USSR, he was already thinking of exterminating the Jewish population. Special groups called *Einzatsgruppen* ("task forces" in English) were established with the task of shooting as many Jews as possible in the newly-acquired Eastern territories. In the space of a few months, hundreds of thousands - possibly up to one million - people were killed. However, this method was considered too inefficient, and a meeting was planned for January 1942 in Berlin to find a definitive solution to the problem. The discussions focussed on organised extermination of any Jews who found themselves on Nazi-occupied territory. They were to be arrested and deported to the camps which had been built in Poland, where the weakest among them would be sent directly to the gas chambers, while the others worked themselves to death, literally. This system came into force in the following months and saw several million Jews and Tziganes deported and executed. This genocide would come to be known as the Holocaust and would last until the end of the war in 1945 when the camps were finally liberated.

IN THE HEAT OF BATTLE

The year 1942 was a decisive year for the Third Reich. Determined to defeat the USSR before it was too late, Hitler launched a new major offensive in the Caucasus and Stalingrad. Just when everything seemed to be going well and the German troops were close to seizing Stalingrad and its oil reserves, the Soviet troops regained the upper hand and proceeded to wipe out the German presence.

In Africa, the British blocked and defeated Erwin Rommel (German field marshal, 1891-1944) in El Alamein while the Americans penetrated Morocco and Algeria. While Hitler initially ordered resistance on all fronts, he was eventually forced allow the evacuation of the most dangerous areas given the formidable threat they faced. The Caucasus was abandoned and the *Afrikakorps* - the German divisions sent to Africa - took refuge in Tunisia.

In May 1943, the Allies liberated all of Africa, conquered Sicily and invaded Italy where Mussolini was arrested. Hitler launched one last offensive in Russia during summer near to Koursk, but this, yet again, was a failure.

In 1944, the Allied air forces managed to establish control over European airspace, forcing German troops to retreat on all fronts. In June, the Allies led landing operations in Normandy, France in a plan known as Operation Overlord and began to liberate mainland Europe little by little. By the end of the year, they had reached Berlin, where Hitler proceeded to lock himself in his bunker before committing suicide on 30 April 1945.

IMPACT

At both a domestic and international level, Nazism and the war it provoked left a permanent mark on history.

Following the war, Germany suffered greatly and virtually disappeared. Not only was the country in ruin alongside the rest of Europe, it was divided into different zones occupied by Allied forces from the USA, Britain, France and the USSR meaning no overall governance was possible. The Eastern territories were annexed to Poland.

The occupying forces introduced denazification policies, aiming to try all the regime's collaborators and ban them from public office in the case of German institutional reconstruction. However, relations between the Western Allies and the Soviets rapidly deteriorated and both camps put an end to this cooperative system in order to use the most valuable former Nazis for their own interests and to establish a new German government in each side's occupied zone. In the West, the Federal Republic of Germany was established by the Allies while the German Democratic Republic was established in the East. Germany would not be reunified until 1990.

At an international level, the end of the war gave rise to several important developments:

- A system of international law was established through the Nuremberg Trials (20 November 1945 – 1 October 1946) which saw those principally responsible for Nazi atrocities who were still alive put to trial for crimes newly-defined for that exact purpose - crimes against humanity and genocide.
- A new organisation which aimed to secure peace among states - the United Nations - was created, since its predecessor the League of Nations had proven ineffective in preventing conflict. The new United Nations had greater means at its disposal.
- Dominant European powers were replaced by two global superpowers - the USSR and the USA. From then on, the world would become bipolar, divided into two antagonistic blocs and heralding the start of what would be known as the Cold War.
- The international community recognised Israel as a state. In light of the Nazis' attempt to exterminate the entire Jewish population, it was agreed that the only way to shield this group from further prosecution was to create a state capable of accommodating it.

SUMMARY

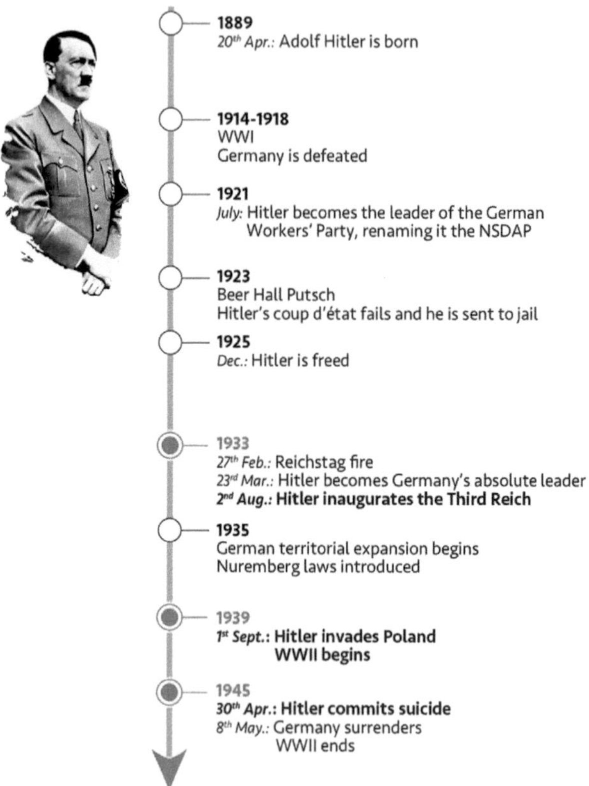

- The formerly homeless failed artist and WWI veteran Adolf Hitler joins a small nationalist party in 1919 and quickly rises through its ranks. In the space of a few years, he transforms it into one of Germany's leading political entities. He develops an ideology founded on German racial supremacy and the elimination of all undesirables, particularly Jews. His overall plan is to take power, seek revenge for the humiliations of the Treaty of Versailles and install a totalitarian regime.

- In 1933, he achieves this goal. He quickly puts his plans into action and he turns Germany into a dictatorship where he is the uncontested leader through fiercely repressive policies. Once his power is consolidated, he begins a programme of territorial expansion and reclaims some of the former German Empire's territories, lost in 1919. He establishes a military alliance with Japan and Italy.

- In 1939, Hitler orders an attack on Poland which prompts the beginning of WWII. His armies go from strength to strength in the first years of the conflict, defeating France, occupying vast areas of mainland Europe and pushing the USSR to the edge of collapse.

- However, things gradually begin to change in 1942. The USA becomes more and more involved in the conflict and the USSR fights back. In May 1945, Germany is defeated and Hitler kills himself in his Berlin bunker.

- Despite its eventual defeat, during the war years Hitler's regime effected the biggest programme of ethnic cleansing Europe has ever known.

We want to hear from you!
Leave a comment on your online library
and share your favourite books on social media!

FIND OUT MORE

BIBLIOGRAPHY

- Bernard, N. (2010) Hitler, un stratège incompétent ? *Ligne de Front. Guerres mondiales. Histoire des conflits du XX siècle*. Aix-en-Provence: Caraktère. pp. 16-35
- Broszkat, M. (2012) *L'État hitlérien. L'origine et l'évolution des structures du Troisième Reich*. Paris: Pluriel.
- Hughes, M. and Mann, C. (2005) *L'histoire du IIIe Reich*. Belgium: Chantecler.
- Kersaudy, F. (2011) *Qui était-il ? Hitler sans masque*. Histoire de la dernière guerre. 1939-45, au jour le jour. Aix-en-Provence: Caraktère. Volume 14.
- Laurent, B. (2008) Les derniers jours d'Hitler. *Axe et Alliés. 1939-1945, un monde en guerre*. Éguilles: Éditions du Paldin. pp. 38-67.
- Richardot, P. (2007) Hitler le chef de guerre. *Axe et Alliés 1939-1945, un monde en guerre*. Éguilles: Éditions du Paldin. pp. 36-63.
- Rosenblaum, R. (1998) *Pourquoi Hitler ? Enquête sur l'origine du mal*. Paris: JC Lattès.
- Sandoz, G. (1980) *Ces Allemands qui ont défié Hitler. Histoire de la résistance allemande*. Paris: Pygmalion/ Gérard Watelet.
- Shirer, W. (1967) *Le IIIe Reich*. Paris: Stock.
- Toland, J. (1978) *Adolf Hitler*. Paris: Pygmalion/Gérard Watelet.

ADDITIONAL SOURCES

- Hitler, A. (2007) Mein Kampf. New York: White Wolf.
- Kershaw, I. (2010) Hitler. New York: W. W. Norton & Company.
- Rees, L. (2013) The Dark Charisma of Adolf Hitler. Croydon: Ebury Press.

ICONOGRAPHIC SOURCES

- Portrait of Adolf Hitler, dated 1933. © Bundesarchiv.
- Photo of Hitler and other German soldiers during WWI. Royalty-free reproduction picture.
- NSDAP meeting in 1930, attended by Hitler. © Bundesarchiv.
- German troops return to Berlin. © German federal archives.
- SA troops saluting Hitler in 1932. © Bundesarchiv.
- SA troops parading in front of Hitler in 1935. Royalty-free reproduction picture.
- Hitler posing with two children. © Charles Overstreet.
- The invasion of Poland, September 1939. © Press Agency Photographer.

IMPROVE YOUR GENERAL KNOWLEDGE

IN A BLINK OF AN EYE !

www.50minutes.com